PLAY-DOH PIONEER

Joseph McVicker

LEE SLATER

Checkerboard Library

An Imprint of Abdo Publishing
abdopublishing.com

abdopublishing.com

Published by Abdo Publishing, a division of ABDO, PO Box 398166, Minneapolis, Minnesota 55439. Copyright © 2016 by Abdo Consulting Group, Inc. International copyrights reserved in all countries. No part of this book may be reproduced in any form without written permission from the publisher. Checkerboard Library™ is a trademark and logo of Abdo Publishing.

Printed in the United States of America, North Mankato, Minnesota
102015
012016

THIS BOOK CONTAINS
RECYCLED MATERIALS

Content Developer: Nancy Tuminelly
Design and Production: Mighty Media, Inc.
Series Editor: Paige Polinsky
Cover Photos: Steve Carlin Papers, di_05811, The Dolph Briscoe Center for American History, The University of Texas at Austin (center); Mighty Media (border)
Interior Photos: Alamy, p. 27; AP Images, p. 15; Courtesy of the Library of Congress, p. 17; Courtesy of The Strong®, Rochester, New York, pp. 24, 29; Getty Images, pp. 19, 25; Juliet McVicker, pp. 5, 6, 7, 11, 23, 26, 28; Shutterstock, pp. 9, 13, 20, 21, 29

Library of Congress Cataloging-in-Publication Data
Names: Slater, Lee, 1969- author.
Title: Play-doh pioneer : Joseph McVicker / by Lee Slater.
Description: Minneapolis, Minnesota : ABDO Publishing Company, [2016] |
    Series: Toy trailblazers | Includes index.
Identifiers: LCCN 2015030431 | ISBN 9781624039782
Subjects: LCSH: McVicker, Joseph, 1930-1991--Juvenile literature. | Play-Doh
    (Toy)--History--Juvenile literature. | Toy industry--Juvenile literature.
    | Inventors--Biography--Juvenile literature. |
    Businessmen--Biography--Juvenile literature.
Classification: LCC T40.M45 S53 2016 | DDC 338.4/768872092--dc23
LC record available at http://lccn.loc.gov/2015030431

CONTENTS

Chapter 1

Born into the BUSINESS

Joseph McVicker was born on September 9, 1930, in Cincinnati, Ohio. His father, Cleophus "Cleo" McVicker, came from a family of Scottish **immigrants**. Irma, Joseph's mother, was an immigrant too. She left Austria for the United States when she was six years old.

Cleo McVicker and his brother Noah McVicker ran a company called Kutol Products. The company made soaps and other cleaning supplies. Noah was the plant manager and product developer. Cleo focused on sales.

In 1928, Cleo and Irma had a daughter, Ruth. The family business was doing well at the time. However, when Joseph was born two years later, many companies were entering the soap-making business. Competition was fierce.

FUN FACT

National Play-Doh Day is September 16, a week after Joseph's birthday.

Irma McVicker poses with her children, Joseph (*left*) and Ruth (*right*).

As a young man, Joseph joined the family business. A changing economy had caused the company's sales to decrease. But Joseph had an idea for a new product that would make the business more successful than ever. That product was Play-Doh, the world-famous toy!

Chapter 2

A CURIOUS Child

As a child, Joseph was creative and **introverted**. He asked many questions and wanted to understand the world around him. From Joseph's earliest days, he wondered about people, life, and **spirituality**. He spent a lot of time listening to music and reading.

Joseph's mother understood her son's quiet, artistic nature. But Joseph's father did not. Cleo was outgoing and active in sports. Joseph was more interested in reading than playing sports. But he did learn to play golf from his father, who was an excellent golfer.

Despite their differences, Joseph (*right*) worked hard to earn his father's approval.

Joseph posing in his Culver Military Academy uniform. The school emphasized discipline and leadership.

After he completed elementary school in 1944, Joseph went to **boarding school**. He attended Culver Military Academy in Culver, Indiana, for four years. The demanding military life was difficult for Joseph. It didn't suit his creative nature. The teachers punished him because he was left-handed. At that time, being left-handed was seen as a flaw. But Joseph wanted his parents to be proud of him. So he buried his **passions**, worked very hard, and did well.

Chapter 3

Growing PAINS

At 18 years of age, Joseph started attending Brown University in Providence, Rhode Island. He was the first in his family to attend college. And he would finally get to study things that interested him!

Joseph took classes in theater, poetry, and literature. He was also still interested in **spiritual** ideas. He wanted answers to big questions, such as the meaning of life.

During his **sophomore** year, Joseph heard about a weekend **workshop** in Kentucky. Thomas Merton, a scholar and priest, was teaching the workshop. Joseph made plans to go. But his father wanted to talk to him about the event first.

Cleo was a pilot and owned his own plane. He took off from Cincinnati to visit Joseph. But he never made it. His plane crashed and he was killed on November 3, 1949.

Joseph's mother, Irma, inherited Kutol Products when Cleo died. She continued to work with Noah. She also hired Bill Rhodenbaugh.

Joseph attended one of the highest-ranking colleges in the United States.

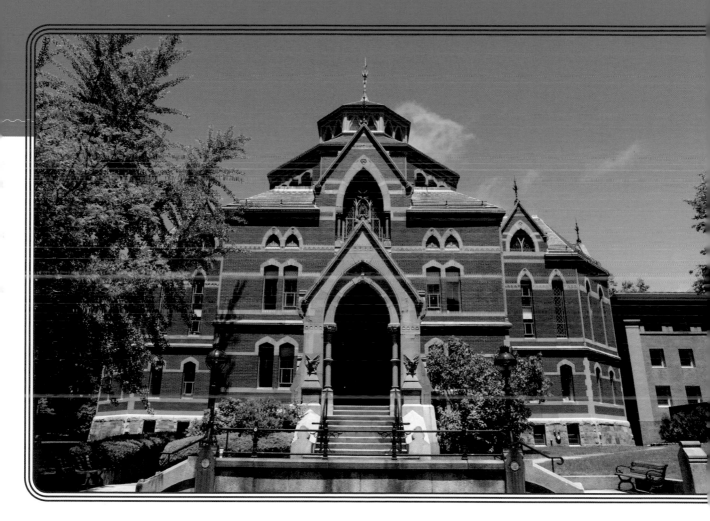

Rhodenbaugh was married to Irma's daughter Ruth. So, the business stayed in the family.

Chapter 4

LIFE GOES ON

Cleo's death was a terrible loss for both the family and the company. Joseph was heartbroken and grieved for several months. But when he returned to college, he felt a new sense of freedom. Joseph no longer had to seek his father's approval. He could follow his own path.

While taking a Shakespeare course, Joseph met Harriet Schwindt. They got married on December 20, 1951. The following spring, they graduated and moved to Cincinnati. Their first child was born on November 30, 1952. Joseph and Harriet named her Juliet.

The good news didn't last for long. A month after Juliet's birth, Joseph was **diagnosed** with a rare form of **cancer**. Joseph and Harriet traveled to New York City to meet with expert doctors. Joseph had an operation that lasted almost eight hours. The doctors discovered more cancer, but they couldn't remove it. They estimated Joseph had only two months to live and sent him back

FUN FACT

Joseph and Harriet fell in love while reading Shakespeare's *Romeo and Juliet*. It was the inspiration for their first child's name.

Both Joseph and Harriet performed in Brown University's musical productions.

home. Joseph decided to try a risky **radiation therapy**. It left him with severe burns, but it worked. Joseph was going to live.

Chapter 5

A Family LEGEND

While Joseph was recovering from his illness, he considered joining the family business. Its best-selling product was no longer in demand, and the company was in trouble. Back in 1933, this same product had saved the company.

In the 1930s, people heated their homes with coal. The smoke left **soot** on their walls. Kroger Foods, a large grocery store **chain**, wanted an excellent wall-cleaning product. Cleo convinced them to place a huge order with Kutol Products. But the product didn't exist yet!

Noah got to work inventing. Soon he had a great product for cleaning walls. They called it Kutol Wall Cleaner. The cleaner was thick like clay and didn't damage wallpaper. Its main ingredients were water, salt, and flour.

The big order was delivered to the Kroger Company on time. Kroger officials liked the product so well that they ordered thousands of cases! Cleo's boldness and Noah's creativity had saved the company from failure. The McVicker family enjoyed a time of great financial success.

Today, we still burn coal. But now we know the smoke contributes to global warming. So, laws regulate the smoke to make it cleaner.

However, after **World War II**, natural gas and oil replaced coal as a heating fuel. These new fuels didn't leave **soot** on the walls. Before Joseph joined the company, sales of Kutol Wall Cleaner dropped and profits went down. Now it was Joseph's chance to come up with a solution.

Chapter 6

A BIG IDEA

The idea for Play-Doh began taking shape in a classroom. Joseph's sister-in-law, Kay Kufall, was a schoolteacher. She told Joseph that Kutol Wall Cleaner made great modeling clay!

Kufall had read a magazine article that suggested using wall cleaner in the classroom. Kufall's students made holiday ornaments from the soft, **pliable** material. After the clay hardened, the students painted the ornaments. It was a fun and successful art project. Other teachers used the clay in their classrooms too.

Kufall's story gave Joseph an idea. He would sell his family's wall cleaner as a toy! Juliet McVicker described her father as "the **ultimate** think-outside-the-box person."

Before Joseph could put his idea into action, he had to do some **market** research. He tested the clay in different schools around the Cincinnati area. The kids and teachers loved it!

FUN FACT

Because Play-Doh is nontoxic, it won't hurt kids if they taste it.

Today's students still enjoy
using Play-Doh in the classroom.

Joseph knew that parents would like the clay too. It didn't stain surfaces such as furniture or floors. It wasn't sticky or crumbly. And because it was nontoxic, it wouldn't harm the children. Kutol Wall Cleaner was about to become a toy!

Chapter 7

BRIGHT NAME,
Bright Future

Joseph was determined to turn the wall cleaner into a best-selling toy. But he needed help to make this dream a reality. He brought in Noah and Rhodenbaugh as business partners. Noah adjusted the wall cleaner **formula** to help it smell better. Now the product just needed a name!

Joseph originally called the clay Kutol's Rainbow Modeling Compound. But Kufall told him the name was too long and boring. When Kufall's husband, Bob, invented the name Play-Doh, it stuck!

In 1955, Joseph introduced Play-Doh at a school supply convention. He planned on selling the clay to schools in bulk. It was packaged in huge containers.

But after the convention, Kutol Products received a major **retail** order. The Woodward & Lothrop department store in Washington, DC,

FUN FACT

Rainbow Craft's original cans contained 1½ pounds (0.7 kg) of Play-Doh!

Woodward & Lothrop operated department stores throughout the mid-Atlantic United States.

wanted to sell Play-Doh! This meant parents could buy Play-Doh for their kids to use at home. So, the company decided to package Play-Doh in smaller containers.

In 1956, Joseph and Noah started Rainbow Crafts Company, Inc. This new business was a **subsidiary company** of Kutol Products. Rainbow Crafts introduced seven-ounce (207 mL) cans of Play-Doh sold in packages of three. Soon, stores from all over the country were placing orders. Play-Doh was a success in schools and homes across the nation!

Chapter 8

PRODUCT Placement

Before 1957, Play-Doh was only available in white. Joseph realized it would be even more fun if Play-Doh came in different colors. The first three Play-Doh colors were red, blue, and yellow. Kids could blend these **primary colors** to make a whole rainbow!

The company needed to tell **consumers** about this new development. But the new **product line** had been expensive to create. Rainbow Crafts didn't have any money left for commercials or magazine ads. Joseph needed a creative way to spread the word.

At the time, *Captain Kangaroo* was the most popular children's show. Joseph boldly walked right into the television studio and onto the show's set. He showed the colorful Play-Doh to Bob Keeshan, who played Captain Kangaroo. Keeshan loved it. He wanted to use it on his show!

FUN FACT

Red is the most popular color of Play-Doh.

Captain Kangaroo (*left*) and Mr. Green Jeans (*right*), characters from *Captain Kangaroo*. The television show ran for a record-breaking 29 years.

Showing a product in a movie or television show is called product placement. This effective form of advertising is usually quite expensive. But Joseph and Keeshan made a deal. If Captain Kangaroo used Play-Doh every week, Keeshan would earn a commission. Sales went crazy as kids around the country saw the new Play-Doh. By the end of the year, Joseph was a millionaire.

Chapter 9

THE PLAY-DOH
Recipe

Today's Play-Doh uses the same ingredients found in the original Kutol Wall Cleaner. But in 1957, Joseph hired Dr. Tien Liu to improve the product. Liu's additional ingredients let kids use the same dough over and over. It didn't harden as quickly as the original Play-Doh.

Making Play-Doh remains a simple process. First, large mixers stir all of the ingredients together. Water heated to about 220 degrees Fahrenheit (104.4°C) is then blended into the mixture. The ingredients are mixed until the flour thickens. This can take up to 30 minutes.

Today there are more than 45 Play-Doh colors.

Recipe for Fun

FLOUR AND WATER are blended together to make the basic dough.

COLOR makes the off-white dough a lot more fun!

WAXY STARCH keeps the dough **pliable**.

ALUMINUM SULFATE stiffens the dough. Its bitter taste is meant to keep kids from eating the dough.

SALT binds up any excess water so the dough won't be too soft or runny.

MINERAL OR VEGETABLE OIL keeps the dough moist. It also keeps it from getting too sticky.

THE FRAGRANCE is rumored to contain some vanilla. The actual ingredients are top secret.

Chapter 10

PARENTING
and Patents

During the late 1950s and early 1960s, Joseph and Harriet had **three** more children. Jack was born on August 30, 1955. Mary was born on June 27, 1959. And Joe was born on June 4, 1964. The McVicker kids grew up playing with Play-Doh. So did their friends and neighbors. According to Juliet, "Anytime anyone came to the house, they played with Play-Doh!"

Rainbow Crafts had created an instant classic toy. Now they needed to get a **patent**. This would protect their legal rights to Play-Doh. It would prevent anyone from stealing the product **formula**. Joseph and Noah filed for a patent on May 17, 1960.

Soon after filing the patent, Joseph made a big decision. Rainbow Crafts was now successful enough to stand on its own. It was time to split from its **parent company**. Joseph and Noah

FUN FACT

A ball made of all the Play-Doh ever created would weigh more than 700 million pounds (317 million kg).

took control of Rainbow Crafts and Play-Doh. Rhodenbaugh remained
the head of Kutol Products. Despite the separation, the two companies
still did business together. Kutol Products packaged Rainbow Crafts
merchandise along with making cleaning supplies.

Chapter 11

The Shape of SUCCESS

By 1964, Rainbow Crafts was shipping more than 1 million Play-Doh cans per year. The company began exporting Play-Doh to England, France, and Italy. Kids all over the world were playing with Play-Doh!

On January 25, 1965, Noah and Joseph were awarded US **patent** #3,167,440. The Play-Doh **formula** was now protected. Sales were strong and improving all the time. Now that Joseph had launched a successful product, he was ready for something new. In 1965, he sold Rainbow Crafts to

FUN FACT

The Play-Doh **mascot** is named Play-Doh Pete.

General Mills bought other toy companies after Rainbow Crafts. One of these, Kenner Products, released the Easy-Bake Oven in 1963.

food manufacturer General Mills. It was General Mills' first experience in the toy industry. They paid $3 million dollars for the Play-Doh **brand** and **formula**.

After selling the company, Joseph retired from life as a businessman. He began attending Harvard Divinity School. His daughter Juliet said it was part of his lifelong inquiry. He was still searching for answers to **spiritual** questions.

Chapter 12

LIFE AFTER
Play-Doh

Joseph graduated from Harvard on June 13, 1968. But he didn't think his education was complete. Joseph was still interested in life's big mysteries. He was especially interested in world religions. After graduating, he decided to continue his studies on his own.

Joseph traveled around the world on a **spiritual** quest. He went to Europe and Asia. He talked to people everywhere he went, and learned from them. Juliet said, "He was very curious and open to seeing what was out there."

Joseph shaped a way to play that has lasted for more than 60 years.

Stamps, stencils, and other accessories make Play-Doh even more fun.

Joseph lived to age 60. He died on April 2, 1991, in Monterey, California. Twenty years later, *TIME* magazine included Play-Doh on its list of "All-TIME 100 Greatest Toys." Hasbro, one of the world's largest toy makers, now owns the Play-Doh **brand**. And more than 2 billion cans have been sold since the toy's invention.

Joseph gave the world a magnificent gift during his lifetime. He gave children the opportunity to create, explore, and experiment. Thanks to Joseph's eye for opportunity, the world of play will never be the same.

FUN FACT

Play-Doh was admitted into the National Toy Hall of Fame in 1998.

TIMELINE

1927

Cleophus and Noah McVicker begin running Kutol Products.

1949

Cleophus dies in a plane crash on November 3.

1955

Joseph tests Kutol Wall Cleaner in schools.

1930

Joseph McVicker is born on September 9 in Cincinnati, Ohio.

1951

Joseph McVicker and Harriet Schmidt are married on December 20.

FUN FACT

A fragrance company called Demeter makes
a Play-Doh-scented cologne.

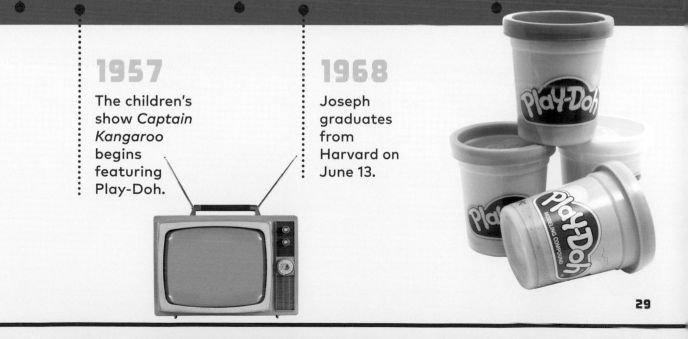

1956

Joseph and Noah
create Rainbow
Crafts, Inc.

1965

Joseph sells Rainbow
Crafts to General
Mills before retiring.

1991

Hasbro, Inc.,
purchases the
Play-Doh brand.
Joseph dies on
April 2 in Monterey,
California.

1957

The children's
show *Captain
Kangaroo*
begins
featuring
Play-Doh.

1968

Joseph
graduates
from
Harvard on
June 13.

boarding school – a school that students may live in during the year.

brand – a category of products made by a particular company and all having the same company name.

cancer – any of a group of often deadly diseases marked by harmful changes in the normal growth of cells. Cancer can spread and destroy healthy tissues and organs.

chain – a group of stores that is owned by the same company and sells similar products.

consumer – a person who buys and uses products and services.

diagnose – to recognize something, such as a disease, by signs, symptoms, or tests.

formula – a combination of specific amounts of different ingredients or elements.

immigrant – a person who enters another country to live.

introvert – a shy person who does not share his or her thoughts or feelings easily.

market – a particular type of people who might buy something.

mascot – a person, animal, or object that is supposed to bring good luck to a team or an organization.

merchandise – goods that are bought or sold.

parent company – a company that controls the management and production of another company.

passion – something one feels very strongly about.

WEBSITES

To learn more about Toy Trailblazers, visit **booklinks.abdopublishing.com**. These links are routinely monitored and updated to provide the most current information available.

patent – the exclusive right granted to a person to make or sell an invention. This right lasts for a certain period of time.

pliable – easily bent or shaped.

primary colors – red, yellow, and blue, which can be mixed to make all the other colors.

product line – a group of related products developed and manufactured by one company.

radiation therapy – the treatment of disease, such as cancer, with X-rays or other forms of radiant energy.

retail – of or having to do with the sale of goods directly to customers.

soot – a black, powdery material formed from burning coal, wood, oil, or other fuel.

sophomore – of or related to the second year of high school or college.

spiritual – of or having to do with religion.

subsidiary company – a company that is owned or controlled by a larger company.

ultimate – greatest or best.

workshop – a meeting where a group of people discuss, learn about, or practice a certain skill.

World War II – from 1939 to 1945, fought in Europe, Asia, and Africa. Great Britain, France, the United States, the Soviet Union, and the allies were on one side. Germany, Italy, Japan, and their allies were on the other side.